Buddys World Alphabet and Coloring BOOK

Buddy

B

Hi Kids, Lets have some FUN !
Color with me and all your new friends.

A is for Alligator

A

ALLIGATOR

A a

B

B is for Bumble Bee

B

Buddys Practice Sheet

B b

C is for Cat

Buddys Practice Sheet

C CAT

C c

D is for Dog

Dd

DOG

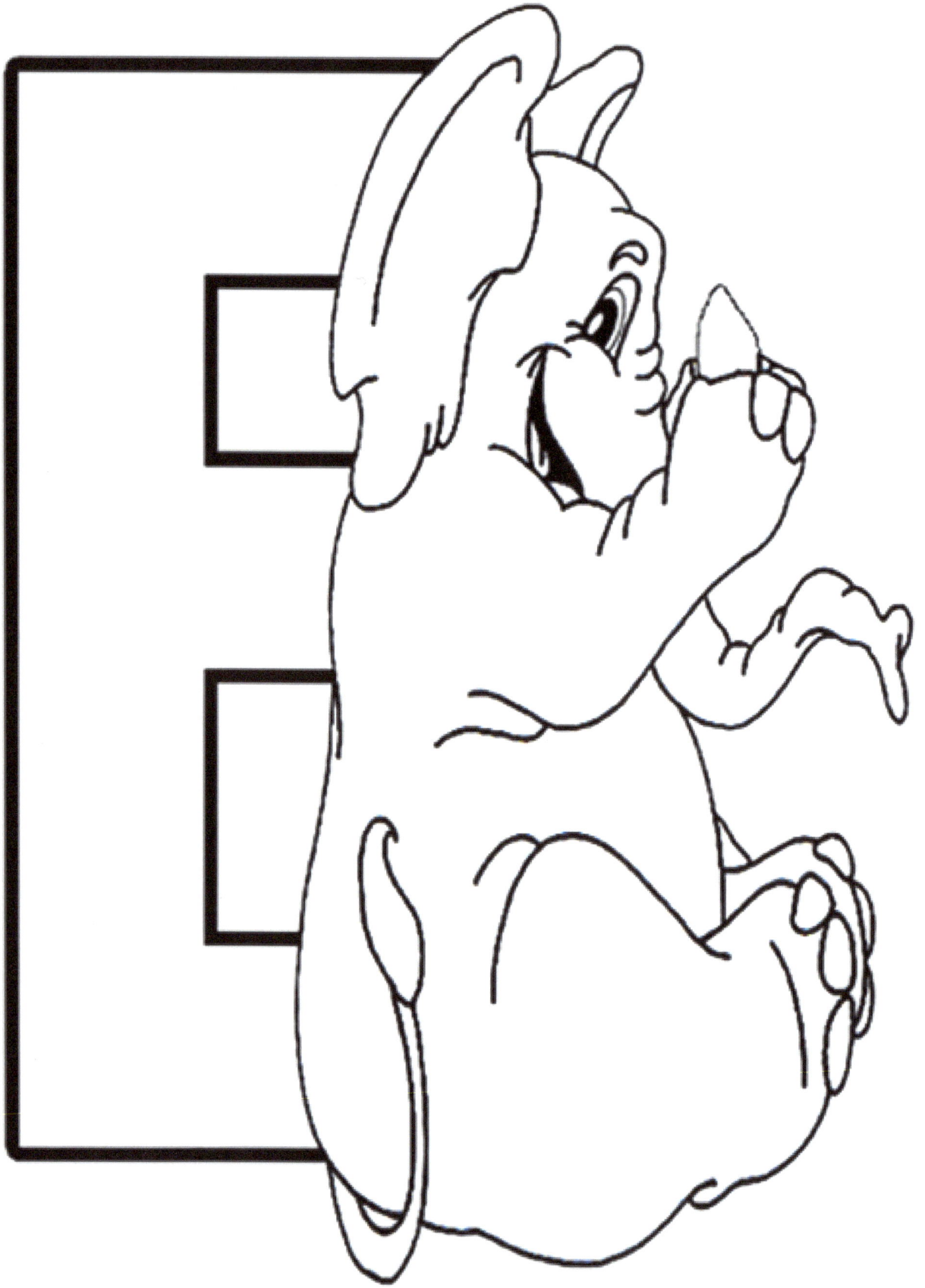

E is Elephant

E

ELEPHANT

Ee

F is for Frog

FROG

Buddys Practice Sheet

Ff

G is for Giraffe

G

GIRAFFE

Gg

H

H is for Honey

H

HONEY

Hh

I is for Insect

I i

J is for Jackrabbit

J

JACKRABBIT

Buddys Practice Sheet

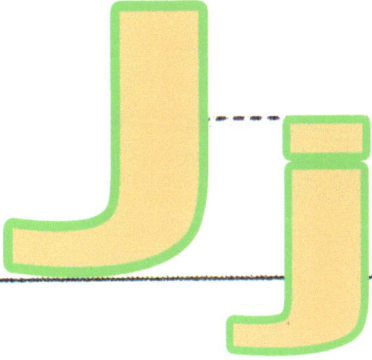

J j

K is for Kangaroo

Kangaroo

Kk

L is for Love

Buddys Practice Sheet

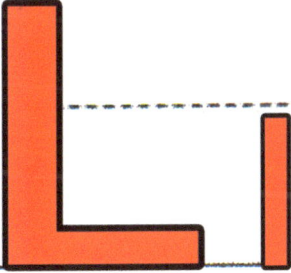

M is for Mice

Mm

N is for Nest

N NEST

Nn

O is for Octopus

Buddys Practice Sheet

OCTOPUS

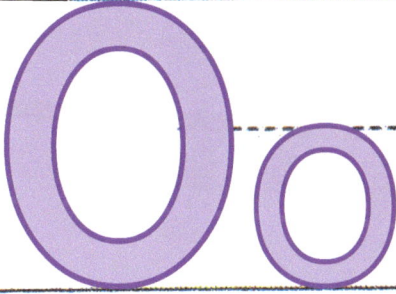

Oo

P is for Pig

P

Buddys Practice Sheet

Pp

Q is for Queen

Qq

R is for Racoon

R r

S is for Seal

S s

T is for Tiger

Buddys Practice Sheet

TIGER

T t

U is for Umbrella

Buddys Practice Sheet

UMBRELLA

U u

V is for Violin

VIOLIN

Vv

W is for Walrus

W

WALRUS

Buddys Practice Sheet

Ww

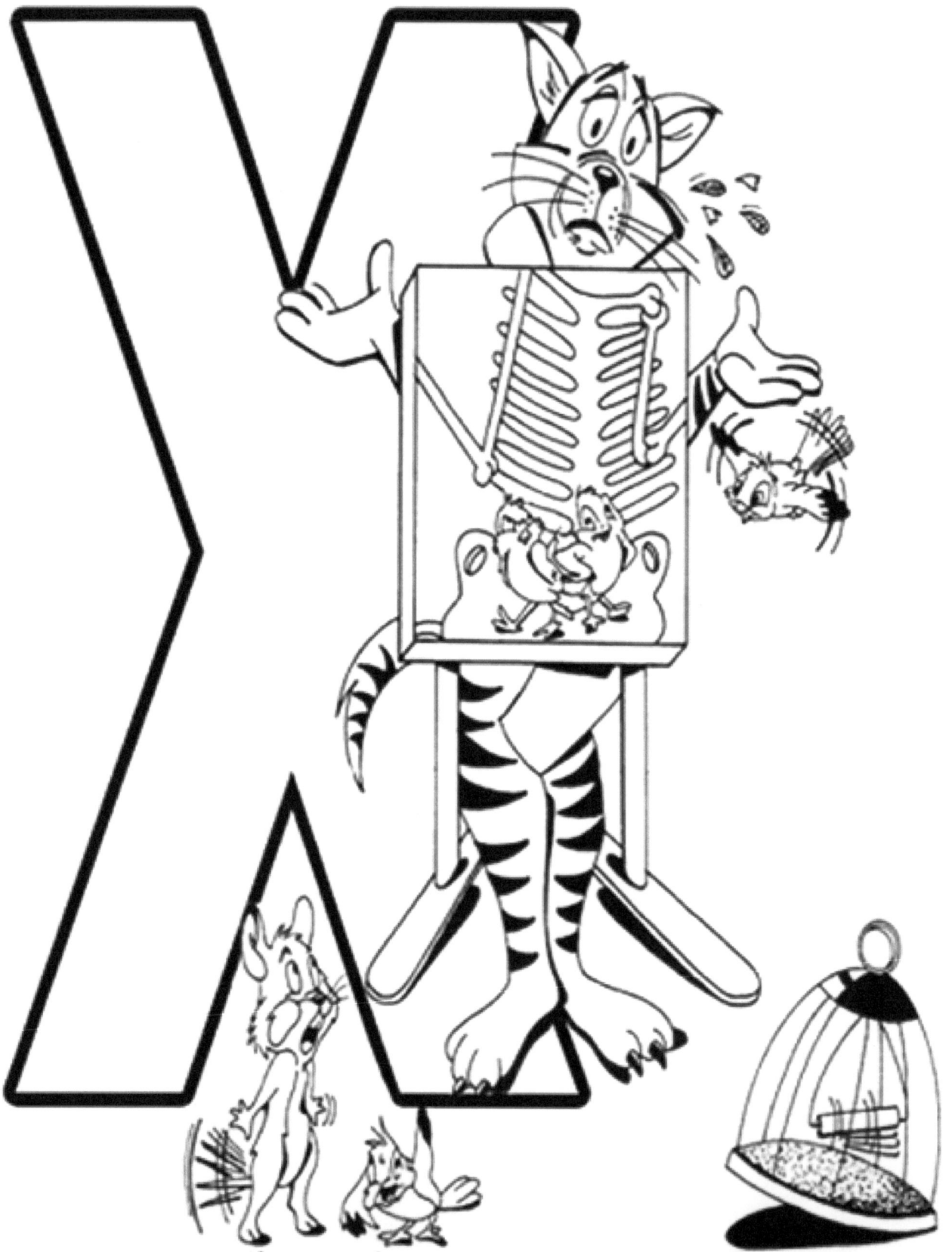

X is for X Ray

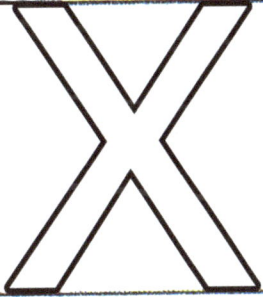

X-RAY

X x

Y is for Yellow

Y

YELLOW

Y y

Z is for Zebra

Zz

BUDDY BEE

I would like to thank all my friends for their help in putting this book together. Have fun and Hapbee coloring ! Buddy Bee